Note to Parents and Teachers

The READING ABOUT: STARTERS series introduces key science vocabulary to young children while encouraging them to discover and understand the world around them. The series works as a set of graded readers in three levels.

LEVEL 2: BEGIN TO READ ALONE follows guidelines set out in the National Curriculum for Year 2 in schools. These books can be read alone or as part of guided or group reading. Each book has three sections:

• Information pages that introduce key words. These key words appear in bold for easy recognition on pages where the related science concepts are explained.
• A lively story that recalls this vocabulary and encourages children to use these words when they talk and write.
• A quiz and index ask children to look back and recall what they have read.

Questions for Further Investigation

RAIN OR SHINE explains key concepts about WEATHER. Here are some suggestions for further discussion linked to questions on the information spreads:

p. 5 *What words would you use to describe the weather today?* Encourage children to use a wide vocabulary, e.g. windy, warm, freezing, cloudy, rainy, icy, frosty, stormy, sunny.

p. 7 *How does sunny weather make you feel?* Encourage children to describe physical effects, e.g. warm on skin, bright in eyes, and emotional, e.g. happy, cheerful.

p. 9 *What happens when the Sun appears from behind a cloud?* Air gets warmer, colours become brighter. Warn children never to look directly at the Sun.

p. 11 *What keeps you dry in the rain?* e.g. waterproof clothing such as a plastic coat or hat, wellington boots and an umbrella. Ask children to think about what they might wear in extreme weather, e.g. in the desert, in a rainforest, or at the North Pole.

p. 13 *What games or sports do people play on snow or ice?* e.g. ice skating, ice hockey, skiing, snowboarding! Ask children to describe own experiences, e.g. sledging/skiing.

p. 15 *Why do people hang out their washing on windy days?* The wind helps to dry clothes.

p. 19 *What should you do in a storm to keep safe?* Stay indoors if possible. Branches from trees may be blown down by strong winds. Avoid standing under trees especially if there is lightning. If you're in a car, make sure the windows are rolled up.

p. 23 *What animals live in a desert? What lives in a rainforest?* Desert animals include camels, snakes, lizards and foxes. More types of animal live in a rainforest than anywhere else, such as gorillas, monkeys, birds, snakes, frogs, butterflies and beetles.

ADVISORY TEAM

Educational Consultant
Andrea Bright – Science Co-ordinator, Trafalgar Junior School, Twickenham

Literacy Consultant
Jackie Holderness – former Senior Lecturer in Primary Education, Westminster Institute, Oxford Brookes University

Series Consultants
Anne Fussell – Early Years Teacher and University Tutor, Westminster Institute, Oxford Brookes University

David Fussell – C.Chem., FRSC

CONTENTS

© Aladdin Books Ltd 2006

Designed and produced by
Aladdin Books Ltd
2/3 Fitzroy Mews
London W1T 6DF

First published in 2006
in Great Britain
by Franklin Watts
338 Euston Road
London NW1 3BH

Franklin Watts Australia
Hachette Children's Books
Level 17/207 Kent Street
Sydney NSW 2000

ISBN 978 07496 6845 7 (H'bk)
ISBN 978 07496 7026 9 (P'bk)

A catalogue record for this
book is available from the
British Library.
Dewey Classification: 551.6

All rights reserved

Editor: Sally Hewitt
Designer: Jim Pipe
Series Design: Flick, Book
Design & Graphics

Thanks to:
The pupils of Trafalgar Infants
School, Twickenham, for
appearing as models in this book.

Printed in Malaysia

Photocredits:
*l-left, r-right, b-bottom, t-top,
c-centre, m-middle*
2tl — Scania. 2ml & bl, 3, 5 both,
6b, 7b, 10, 11br, 15b, 23tr, 25m,
26bl, 27ml, 28b, 29b, 31tr, 31bl,
32 — istockphoto.com. 4, 27tr,
30tr — Digital Vision. 6tl, 11t, 13,
14tl, 15tr, 16-17 all, 18-19 all, 20,
22l, 23b, 24br, 26mr, 31mr, 31bc
— Corbis. 7tr — TongRo. 8mr, 9
both, 12tl, 14b, 21l, 22r, 31ml & br
— Photodisc. 8b — Marc Arundale
/Select Pictures. 12b — Stockbyte.
21r — DAJ. 24tl, 25tr, 26tl, 28tr,
29tr — Comstock. 27br — Flat Earth.

WEATHER

Rain or Shine

By
Jim Pipe

Aladdin/Watts
London • Sydney

What is the **weather** today?
Weather can be hot and dry.
Weather can be cold and wet.

The **weather** is what happens in the air, in the **sky** and outside on the ground.

Dry, hot weather

Weather changes all the time.
It affects what we do
and what we wear.

In hot **weather** we wear
clothes that are cool.

In wet **weather** we wear
clothes that keep us dry.

Wet weather

Scientists measure the weather. They tell us what the weather will be like tomorrow or next week.

• What words would you use to describe the weather today?

The **Sun heats** our world.
In the morning the **Sun** rises.
It **heats** up the air and sea.

In the middle of the day,
the **Sun** is hottest.

In the evening, the **Sun** sets.
The air **cools**.

Sunset

This **thermometer** measures how hot and cold the air is.

At 0 degrees Celsius it is very cold.

At 30 degrees Celsius it is hot.

On a hot, sunny day, the sky is often blue.

Thermometer

• How does sunny weather make you feel?

Clouds are made of tiny drops of water. These drops are too small to see.

When the water drops get bigger, a **cloud** turns grey or black.

If you see a dark **cloud**, rain is on its way!

Clouds

8

You can't see far on a foggy day.

Clouds can make the day cooler. They hide the Sun. We can't feel the Sun's warmth as much.

Mist and **fog** are **clouds** that touch the ground.

Mist

• What happens when the Sun appears from behind a cloud?

When water drops fall from clouds, it **rains**.
When it **rains** hard, we say it pours.
When **raindrops** are small, we say it drizzles.

Rainy day

Rain fills rivers, ponds and lakes.
It makes puddles.

Flood

Rain helps plants to grow. Animals need **rain** water to drink.

No **rain** makes plants dry up and die. Too much **rain** creates a **flood**. Streets turn into rivers.

When the Sun shines through raindrops, it makes a rainbow.

• What keeps you dry in the rain?

On a cold day, raindrops can turn to **ice** in the air.

Hailstones are hard lumps of **ice**. Big **hailstones** can even break windows when they fall.

Frost

On a cold night, tiny drops of water turn to **ice**. This is **frost**.

Skiing on snow

When it is very cold, rain turns to **snow**.

Snow covers the ground in a white blanket. It is hard to walk on **snow**, but skis can help you move fast!

Mountain tops are covered in **snow** all year round.

• What games or sports do people play on snow or ice?

A strong wind makes it hard to walk.

Wind is moving air. You feel the **wind** on your skin.

Wind blows clouds across the sky. **Wind** makes waves on the sea.

Waves

The **wind** can make things move.

Wind blows a boat across the water.
Wind blows a kite into the air.

Storm

On some days, the wind blows very hard. This is a **storm**.

A **storm** can bring lots of rain. It can break trees and houses. **Storms** can be very dangerous.

16

Some **storms** make a loud rumbling noise. This noise is called **thunder**.

Sometimes a bright, white light jumps across the sky. This is called **lightning**.

Lightning

A snow storm is called a blizzard.

• *How does windy and stormy weather make you feel?*

A **hurricane** is a giant storm.

Hurricane winds are very, very strong. They can blow down trees and houses. They create giant waves at sea.

Hurricane rains cause floods.

A hurricane is so big it can be seen from space.

Hurricane damage

Tornado

In a **tornado**, air spins
around and around very fast.
Some people call a **tornado** a 'twister'.

A strong **tornado** smashes houses.
It lifts cars into the air.

• What should you do in a storm to keep safe?

The weather **changes** during the year.
These are the **seasons**.

Some parts of the world have two **seasons**,
a wet **season** and a dry **season**.

In the wet **season** it rains and rains.
In the dry **season** there may be no rain.

Dry season

Some parts of the world have four **seasons**.

In spring, it often rains. Summer days are often warm and sunny.

Autumn days may be windy and cool. Winter days are often cold.

Autumn

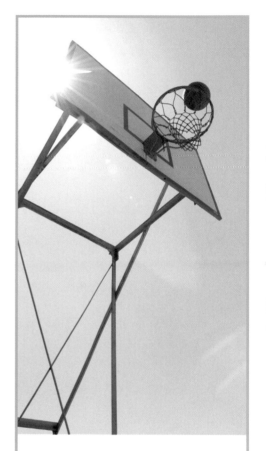

In summer, the Sun is higher in the sky than in winter.

• What is your favourite season?

Weather is different all over the world.

Places near the middle of the Earth
get the most sunshine. They are hottest.

Rainforests are hot and wet.
Deserts are hot and dry.

Desert

Rainforest

22

Places at the ends of the Earth are coldest. They are called the **poles**.

There is ice at the **poles** all year round.

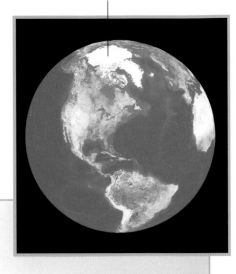

North Pole

Polar bears and seals live near the North **Pole**. Their fur keeps them warm.

• What animals live in a desert? What lives in a rainforest?

STORMY WEATHER

Look out for words
about **weather.**

It is the day of the
school picnic.
The **weather** is hot.
The **Sun** is shining.

Mrs Jackson takes a
picture of her class.

Mia sees **clouds**
floating across the **sky.**

"I think the **weather**
is **changing,**"
says Tom.

"It's going to **rain.**"

24

"Well, I like **clouds**," says Mia.
She looks for shapes in the **clouds**.

"That **cloud** is like you, Tom,"
jokes Mia. "It's got a grumpy face."

"Thick **clouds** can be dangerous," says Tom.
"**Fog** and **mist** make it hard for ships
to see where they are going."

"But a lighthouse shows them the way,"
says Mrs Jackson.

"I love the **Sun**," says Asha. She likes to feel the **heat** of the **Sun** on her skin.

"Too much **Sun** is bad," says Tom.

"The **Sun** shines every day in a **desert**. It's very hot and dry."

"If I was a camel I could live in a **desert**," laughs Asha.

"I like **rain**," says Paula.
"I splash in puddles and
watch the **raindrops** fall."

"Too much **rain** is bad," says Tom.
"In the **rainforest** it **rains** for months.
The forest **floods** in the wet **season**."

"You could have a
house on stilts and
get around in a boat,"
says Mrs Jackson.

"I like **snow**," says Adi.
"It's fun to play in
the **snow**."

"Too much **snow** is bad,"
says Tom. "At the
poles there is always
snow and **ice**."

"We could use dogs and a sled to get
around," says Adi. "That would be fun."

"I like the **wind**," says Alisha.

"When the **wind blows** hard, it is great for flying a kite," she says.

"Wind brings bad **weather**," says Tom. "Like those dark **clouds**."

Suddenly a bolt of **lightning** shoots across the **sky**. **Thunder** rumbles above.

"I love **stormy weather**," says Pete. "Look at that **sky!**"

Everyone runs to the bus.
Pete stays to watch
the **storm**.

The **rain** begins to pour.
Pete runs to the bus.
It's too late. Pete is soaked.

"So Tom was right about the **weather**!"
says Asha. Everyone laughs – even Pete!

Make a chart of the **weather** this week.
You can draw pictures showing each
sort of **weather**.

Monday	Tuesday	Wednesday	Thursday

Friday	Saturday	Sunday

QUIZ

What measures how
hot or cold the air is?

Answer on page 7

What do we call **clouds**
that touch the ground?

Answer on pages 9

What can happen
in a **storm**?

Answer on page 16-17

What sort of weather do
these pictures show?

INDEX